ARTFUL DECORATION

INTERIORS BY FISHER WEISMAN

For Claudia – fondly,
Jeffry Weisman
&
Andrew Fisher

ARTFUL DECORATION

INTERIORS BY FISHER WEISMAN

Foreword by Margaret Russell

Edited by Anthony Iannacci

The Monacelli Press

This book wouldn't have been possible without the truly amazing clients who have grown with us, opened their homes and lives to us, and trusted us to conjure their dreams—often becoming great friends in the process. What an extraordinary gift it is to work with you.

In addition, Andrew Fisher would like to thank Johnny Hallock for giving him a priceless education in the classic art of decorating and Tony Duquette for being a kindred spirit whose friendship and over-the-top style were the catalysts he needed to fuel a fearless imagination.

Jeffry Weisman thanks Matt Kahn for being his toughest critic when he needed it most—in college; Charles Pfister, whose unerring taste and drive for perfection set the standard; and Cynthia Silverstein, for trusting an eager sixteen-year-old to gently lift that first fauteuil from her front seat.

FOREWORD

Interior designers have been making our world a more beautiful place for centuries. But decorators who create magic—whose work transports us to another realm—are rare indeed. Among those geniuses today are Andrew Fisher and Jeffry Weisman of Fisher Weisman.

In their work, sleight of hand and trompe l'oeil abound: A chandelier isn't merely a light fixture; it is an apparition that appears to be made of gilded branches. Kitchen cabinets are inset with smoked-mirror panels that cast glimmering reflections. At the flick of a switch, a bathroom's lyrical, shell-encrusted ceiling fixture becomes an unimaginably glamorous tub-filler; while a dramatic, wall-size collage turns out to be an assemblage of paper coffee filters—stretched flat, subtly dyed, and finely stitched into a vast grid. Even the design duo's most simplistic spaces offer transporting experiences through exquisite accents and the melding of elements both humble and luxe—raw plaster, wool flannel, graphic African mud cloth, and rustic stone mixed with intricately painted faux bois, supple glove leather, sparkling quartz crystals, and sensuous silk velvet.

Over the years, I've published several magazine features on Fisher Weisman's projects, but it's Jeffry and Andrew's own homes that have been the most memorable for me; they are the places that are truly emblematic of their firm's signature style. The swank, sophisticated Nob Hill flat where the two live in San Francisco and the extraordinary estate they built in the Sonoma Valley share an essential quality, a unique balance between practicality and poetry. We all want to live in homes that are comfortable and inviting—but a bit of fantasy never hurts. After all, who doesn't want to live happily ever after?

—Margaret Russell

Editor in Chief, *Architectural Digest*

PREFACE

We've always preferred the old-fashioned moniker *decorator* to the more corporate-sounding *designer,* though in fact our work depends as much on thoughtful planning as it does on creating a gorgeous envelope. The words "design" and "decoration," which follow the company name on our letterhead, sum up what we do quite well.

Andrew approaches our work from an artist's perspective. He studied metalsmithing, drawing, and sculpture at the California College of the Arts and learned the ropes of the decorating business working with the late carriage-trade decorator Johnny Hallock. He looks at rooms the way he looks at canvases: considers the subject and the background, carefully builds a palette of colors, and layers textures to achieve a satisfying whole. His imagination knows no bounds and he delights in creating whimsical fantasy furniture and lighting projects that often find their way into our installations.

I studied art and design as an undergraduate at Stanford and went on to design interiors and furniture first at Skidmore, Owings & Merrill under Charles Pfister and later at Gensler under Orlando Diaz-Azcuy. Returning to the Stanford Graduate School of Business, I earned an MBA before opening my own design practice. My training and education endowed me with a pragmatic approach to design and a solid foundation for operating the business. I'm a detail-oriented designer with a passion for directing projects from planning through installation and I work diligently to achieve the right balance of elements in every composition.

Combining Andrew's artistic yin with my practical yang, we merged our practices in 2000 to create Fisher Weisman. When asked to describe our style to new clients, we often show images of three large apartments we designed in the same luxury tower. All share the same floor plan and finishes, yet the completed interiors bear little resemblance to one another. Each is our vision of the *clients'* style: our visual construct of who they are, what they love, and how they live. Our goal is to get to know our clients and come to understand their requirements and dreams better than they do themselves. This allows us to create deeply personal rooms that will suit them more perfectly and endure longer than they could have imagined.

We've never sought to create a trademark look. Our own homes, several of which are included in these pages, are perhaps the best example of what could be considered our own "style." In these urban and country residences, a layered mix of old and new and moments of formality, fantasy, and simplicity thread together in what strikes us as uniquely our own. In an era of increasingly mass-produced, standardized design, we find ourselves at the other end of the spectrum: spending more time and effort to create the special and handcrafted rather than opting for the quick and convenient, both for our houses and those of our clients.

The lens through which we appreciate and create beauty has been honed and polished by the places we've lived, our travels, the artisans we discover along the way, and the great designers of the past. San Francisco, where we have lived and worked most of our lives, has immersed us in its dressy, grown up version of classic California style. Rooms and furniture arrangements are somewhat relaxed and the essential love of indoor/outdoor living, particularly beyond the city limits, remains intact—but the level of sophistication is high. The grand houses and refined tastes of many clients there have been well suited to our sensibilities and proved a fertile ground to grow and work. Our childhood years—mine in Southern California and Andrew's in the Midwest and deep South—add other dimensions to what we love and how we think. Working in other parts of the country and abroad has further expanded our appreciation for how people live and how to discern what works best in any given locale.

We have always loved to explore. The ability to hop on a plane and wake up immersed in a completely fresh and utterly different culture is a thrill. Andrew spent a year of his childhood living in Brussels and traveling around Europe, and has longed to see new things and discover new places ever since. Studying in Florence during college inspired my love of travel and living abroad that continues today. Many places we've visited have dramatically changed the way we think and see, most notably Africa, Southeast Asia, India, Mexico, the Middle East, and the great capitals of Western Europe. Experiencing the light in Venice and the Sahara forever changed the way we see color. The grand palaces and gardens of France and Italy dazzled us in a completely different way than those of Rajasthan. The stupas of Burma, the temples of Cambodia, and the monuments of Egypt were all magically inspiring in discrete ways. The lessons we have gleaned from each astonishingly beautiful place are akin to learning new visual languages that weave their way into our work over time, adding their distinct dimensions and nuances.

Discovering extraordinary artisans, crafts, and objects old and new is another aspect of world travel we love. The lacquer of Burma and Vietnam, the carved stone of India, blown glass from Murano, Chinese porcelains, Mexican ceramics, Turkish ikats and woven peacock feathers from India are examples of things that have intrigued us and even inspired entire rooms. That's to say that extraordinary craftsmen in the souks and villages affect us just as strongly as treasures from the finest museums and auction houses.

Great designers including Renzo Mongiardino, Tony Duquette, Charles Pfister, Billy Baldwin, Valerian Rybar, John Saladino, and Albert Hadley, to name our favorites, inspired us with their groundbreaking flair, discipline, and elegance. The lessons we learned by studying the best rooms these highly original designers created are endless.

Our work takes us far and wide, both for specific projects and inspiration. In 2011, a trip to the seventeenth-century Spanish colonial town of San Miguel de Allende resulted in the surprise purchase of a house, photographs of which are included in the final chapter of this book. What we expected would be a vacation home in short order became the Latin American outpost of the Fisher Weisman firm. We enjoy immensely the variety that projects in Mexico add to our repertoire. We continue to develop furniture and lighting designs for several manufacturers and have recently created our own home furnishings line named after our San Miguel house, Casa Acanto.

—Jeffry Weisman

San Miguel de Allende, August 2012

NOB HILL PIED-À-TERRE
SAN FRANCISCO, CALIFORNIA

We designed our Nob Hill apartment—one of fifteen in a superb 1920s Louis XVI–style building—with glamorous entertaining in mind.

Elsie de Wolfe consulted on the interiors when the building was first constructed, which explains the quality and authenticity of the period detailing. We configured the dining room from a small entrance hall and several closets; all trim was milled to replicate the original profiles found in the adjacent living room. The woodwork, enhanced with many coats of a deep chocolate Dutch lacquer, frames panels of hand-blown antique mirror; both reflect candlelight to create a dressy, luxurious, nighttime feel. We crafted an outsized, exotic, shell-encrusted lantern to hang over our Lauro dining table and activate the room's tall volume.

When Anthony Hail, the legendary San Francisco decorator, lived in this apartment in the 1970s, he removed the original paneling above the chair rail in the main entertaining space. In this almost perfectly square living room, we replaced the paneling to restore the space's original sense of rhythm and commissioned Karin Wikström to paint all the trim, including original plaster reliefs above the doors, with a *faux-bois* finish that evokes bleached walnut. We then incorporated the antiqued mirror into the newly reconstructed *boiserie*. Both the furniture—including numerous antique French and Russian chairs, which can easily be moved across the bare floors—and the dark, smoky, neutral color scheme were selected to allow flowers, artwork, and accessories to vary its mood depending on the season, event, or even hour.

The master bedroom is a cozy cocoon with walls, drapery, and canopy bed all upholstered in the same English wool; the interior of the bed is lined with creamy Thai silk. The master dressing room replaced a former bedroom, correcting the typical lack of closet space in older apartments. We fashioned the 10-foot-tall shutters with panels from hand-carved teak Indian screens and lacquered them in a creamy white to provide a soft, filtered light as well as privacy.

The edited palette of browns and creams we used throughout the apartment continues into the guest room. This disciplined use of color unifies the spaces, creating flow between rooms.

Anthony Hail, the legendary San Francisco decorator, lived in this apartment in the 1970s; he had removed the original paneling above the chair rail, which has now been replaced and filled with antiqued plate glass. The trim and original plaster reliefs are treated with a *faux-bois* finish to add warmth.

Above: An eighteenth-century Lombardy drop-front desk paired with a fantasy chair embellished by Andrew Fisher. The still-life oil painting and fantasy egg boxes are also created by Fisher.

Opposite: A custom-designed side table has gilded steel legs shaped like twigs and a thick, carved top of limed walnut.

Overleaf left: An eighteenth-century Lucchese table hosts a cut-and-layered glass lamp designed by Fisher Weisman, produced in Murano. The pair of carved stone Tang Dynasty horses is from the estate of John Hallock.

Overleaf right: A corner of the master bedroom features an eighteenth-century Swedish *secrétaire à abattant* and a nineteenth-century faux marquetry Italian chair. A collection of Favrile glass by Louis Comfort Tiffany and a Biedermeier clock sit atop the desk; an eighteenth-century miniature Italian armchair completes the grouping.

Wool flannel lined in silk and a quilted silk bolster cover handmade by Andrew Fisher add opulence to a canopy bed. A large collection of framed costume and set designs by Eugene Berman from the 1940s and 1950s decorate the walls.

Above: A peek into a guest room reveals a bed upholstered in wool flannel with contrasting grosgrain trim, a bedspread of antique African mud cloth, and walls covered in a shagreen-textured vinyl.

Opposite: Teak screens from India act as interior shutters over the tall windows of a master dressing room; white lacquer helps to incorporate them with the rest of the millwork. Barcelona stools add a modern contrast.

SOMA LOFT
SAN FRANCISCO, CALIFORNIA

Andrew Fisher transformed a new-construction duplex loft in the South of Market neighborhood of San Francisco into a highly personal and sophisticated home by altering the original build-out slightly and adding plenty of vibrant accessories.

Using simple blocks of cabinetry, he created a backdrop for the dining room and an entertainment center facing the living area. Upstairs, new closets frame the view from the bedroom and provide much-needed storage. Dark oak floors anchor the volume of the space and add a dash of glamour.

Andrew's fantasy creations fill the space and live comfortably side-by-side with antiques and objects collected on travels. A focal point of the entertaining space is a fanciful secretary he created; it features a canopy of gesso-covered linen, faux coral fretwork, and oyster shells. Four vintage side chairs continue the fantasy theme with his addition of faux coral lattice backs, more oyster shells, and drapery skirts made rigid with layers of gesso and paint. An overscaled quilt he crafted from used coffee filters—a medium adopted out of necessity in art school but one he often returns to today—hangs above the living room sofa.

Moments of complete whimsy punctuate the loft. The chandelier over the dining table, crafted with elements of a vintage Philippine plant hanger, tart tins, wooden dowels, copper toilet tank floats, and countless seashells, sets an exuberant tone just inside the front door. The richly eccentric pieces, both collected and created for the space, make a dramatic effect against the quiet backdrop of an otherwise simple, modern box.

Above: Red mohair chairs and an elaborate shell chandelier by Andrew Fisher endow a small dining room with glamour.

Opposite: Vintage Thai hats adorn a card table of Fisher's creation; the ornateness of their decoration echoes its flamboyant, black-lacquered, shell-encrusted base and gilded pedestal and top. A chair decorated by Fisher completes the vignette.

Previous pages, left: A fantasy secretary by Fisher featuring a canopy of linen dipped in gesso and painted a high-gloss white, faux coral fretwork, and oyster shells becomes a focal point.

Above and opposite: A massive piece of Fisher's art—made from painted and stained coffee filters sewn together—dominates a wall in a living room. Its darker tones play off the stained oak floors that give what was a nondescript, boxlike space a dose of drama and provide a backdrop for an eclectic collection of furnishings and objects.

Above and opposite: A collection of fantasy egg boxes and faux-seaweed candlesticks, both by Fisher, play off the forms of an eighteenth-century French ormolu clock, Thai headdresses, and an eighteenth-century Portuguese mirror—a gift from Tony Duquette.

White-painted temple hangings from Thailand adorn a fantastical linen canopy above a bed. The bedspread is made from African mud cloth and the contrasting trapunto silk quilt was hand sewn by Fisher.

BEAUX-ARTS FLAT
SAN FRANCISCO, CALIFORNIA

Our charge on this project was to harness the elegance inherent in the bones of this 1920s apartment while modernizing the private spaces to meet the needs of a young family.

The apartment had been substantially demolished when our clients found it: all of the floors, many walls, the electrical and plumbing systems, the kitchen and bathrooms, and even the fireplace mantels were gone. We retained most of the original wall locations but updated the space by opening the original master bedroom onto the living room, claiming space that had been a maid's room and bath to create a larger kitchen and family room, and adding a powder room in what had been a hallway.

For the foyer, we commissioned chinoiserie murals—painted on canvas coated with layers of cracked gesso and glazed to appear elegantly aged. New floors of white oak laid in a herringbone pattern feel as if they could be original to the space and draw attention to a dramatic enfilade we created across the full length of the building. Tall pairs of mirror-paneled doors enhance the effect of this enfilade and the height of the rooms. This remarkable public space, with its two antique French fireplaces, can accommodate large cocktail parties and dinners, but also has intimate spots for reading.

The clients' passion for antiques inspired the décor of the public rooms, which are formal yet inviting. The private spaces are far more relaxed and casual.

Above: Faux-bois wall treatments and a custom twig chandelier lend a relaxed-yet-sophisticated air to a dining room.

Opposite: Opening a series of small rooms, raising the height of the existing doorway to the dining room, and adding tall doors with mirror panels to introduce an enfilade helped to create a dramatic space. A nineteenth-century English armchair and a 1940s French side table sit on an antique Serapi rug.

Linen velvet unites a "Schiaparelli" sofa and a pair of slipper chairs by Fisher Weisman. A set of 1940s French consoles with carved, gilded tree bases and marble tops host a pair of ceramic lamps that pick up the upholstery's dark hue. Antique Chinese children's chairs complete the seating arrangement.

Chinese accents spill over into a sitting room, where an antique painted leather chest, "frog" chair, and upholstered sofa designed by Fisher Weisman are paired with a brightly hued antique Serapi rug. The upright, rectilinear forms of an antique map of Paris, a nineteenth-century French drop-front secretary, a nineteenth-century French mantel, and an overscaled mirror complete the room.

Above: New floors of white oak and silk drapery with a subtle *strié* pattern carry into the master bath. A nineteenth-century English side chair punctuates the view through tall French windows.

Opposite: Dark, heavy paneling in the master bedroom is transformed and modernized with the application of a light and airy *faux-bois* finish.

GOLD COAST DUPLEX
CHICAGO, ILLINOIS

For this downtown Chicago apartment with limited natural light, the mandate from our clients was to create a "riot of color."

We treated the walls of the entrance hall and living room with a bold *strié* finish in vibrant coral tones. The trim was painted with a *faux-bois* design in the same rich orange-red hues.

The clients' love of collecting is evident in the living room, where an antique Oushak carpet, a 1940s Venetian mirror, a Biedermeier secretary, a pair of eighteenth-century Swedish chairs, and a rare pair of Maison Baguès side tables decorated with delicate paintings of feathers coalesce to dramatic effect. Additionally, we designed the hand-embroidered borders on the vibrant silk drapery and created a hand-carved settee that incorporates our client's monogram in the fretwork.

Chartreuse dominates the elliptical dining room, which has silk-covered walls, silk taffeta drapery, chairs with tiger-striped silk velvet upholstery whose form subtly references the room's shape, and a signature chandelier and sconces that we crafted especially for the space.

Steve Rugo of Rugo/Raff Ltd. Architects created an inviting family room and kitchen from several awkward rooms, and gave it an updated but traditional look. The breakfast room was added by enclosing part of the patio and is a sunny spot ideal for family meals. A built-in bookcase at one end displays a bit of the client's extensive antique porcelain collection.

Opposite: A bold *strié* wall finish in coral tones announces the apartment's personality to guests in the entry, with help from a 1940s Murano mirror and an eighteenth-century Swedish commode.

Above and overleaf: The coral motif continues into the living room, where the trim is painted with a fantasy *faux-bois* design in the same vibrant coral tones. The custom-designed settee features the client's monogram in its fretwork.

Above and opposite: Oval walls dictated the shape for a custom mahogany-and-brass dining table. The designers also crafted a chandelier of gilded steel frosted with rock crystal, seashells, and strings of crystal beads especially for the space, and designed the sconces in gilded steel and rock crystal for the walls to coordinate as well.

Nestled snugly between the kitchen and the breakfast room, the family room hosts a collection of custom-designed upholstered pieces featuring intricate and unusual details.

Above and opposite: Enclosing a portion of the adjacent terrace created space for a sunny and comfortable breakfast room that is also perfect for intimate family dinners. The owners' extensive and colorful antique porcelain collection creates the decorative focus.

PALM CANYON RETREAT
PALM SPRINGS, CALIFORNIA

Inspired by travels around the world, this couple decided to build a Moroccan-themed house in the desert near Palm Springs. Tichenor & Thorp Architects devised a refined refuge that wraps around a luxurious pool and a garden that perfectly frames a mountain view. We worked closely with the architects to incorporate luxurious materials and details to enhance the house's happy blend of modern lines and antique forms.

Having recently sold a midcentury modern house nearby, the clients were ready for a more "dressed up" décor. Taking cues from the architecture, we developed a scheme for the interior that is inspired by Morocco but contemporary in mood. Luxurious textiles such as linens, chenilles, and tapestry weaves add texture and color to the rooms. In the main entertaining area, we created a hanging constellation of lanterns the clients brought home; it activates the room's tall ceilings and adds visual interest to what is traditionally an overlooked space.

Surprisingly, many of the decorative elements in the house were sourced not from Northern Africa, but from India, including an inset medallion of black and white marble in the entry hall, red sandstone floors laid in varying patterns throughout the house, red sandstone blocks that frame the garden pools, and the white marble fountains that accent the landscape.

The house was built for pure relaxation. Large comfortable spaces indoors, under cover facing the gardens, and in the gardens themselves invite all kinds of diversions. The kitchen is set up for cooking parties and accommodating large events. The master suite is equally generous but intensely private; guest rooms are arranged discreetly around the public rooms.

Above: Indian sandstone floors, a black and white marble medallion inset, and a white-lacquered *mashrabiya* window grille in the entry hall begin the house's exotic theme. The walls are finished with Venetian plaster and textured to emulate stucco.

Opposite: Moroccan-inspired custom consoles in distressed red lacquer punctuate a long hallway and repeat the shape of its Moorish arches.

Overleaf: In the dining area, a Portuguese-style table and chairs and custom-designed sideboards with recessed door panels in a traditional Moorish pattern reinforce the North African theme.

Above: A door rendered almost transparent with large panes of light-colored glass in a simple geometric pattern allows the light from a generous, welcoming bay window beyond to penetrate deep into the house's interior.

Opposite: A collection of Moroccan lanterns with different forms animates a dining area, which flows into an entertainment room.

Painted cabinetry is framed with a lively Moroccan tile backsplash.

Overleaf: The view from the pool pavilion extends through the house and to the mountains beyond.

PACIFIC HEIGHTS PENTHOUSE
SAN FRANCISCO, CALIFORNIA

Our clients fell in love with this unique duplex penthouse in the elegant Pacific Heights neighborhood, recently remodeled from top to bottom by Andrew Skurman, and challenged us to reimagine it for their decidedly modern tastes. Our instinct was to simplify the interiors to create the more contemporary look they had in mind.

To retain the integrity of Skurman's design and fulfill the clients' request for a serene background, we made minor simplifications and enveloped the large space in a palette of creamy whites with soft, matte finishes. In the foyer, we removed pairs of large, formal-feeling columns and replaced a traditional balustrade on the stair with a ribbon of sleek plaster topped with a curved white oak handrail in the same color as the decorative parquet flooring. Similarly, we designed a contemporary mantel in limestone to replace the traditional antique in the living room, and paired custom upholstery and case pieces with stylish vintage elements. We designed modern interpretations of Serapi carpets in cream with a chocolate-brown pattern in the living room and reversed the color scheme in the adjacent dining room to reinforce the mood. The room that gets the most use during the day contains the lighter carpet, and the room that gets the most use at night holds the darker. In the dining room, we removed plaster ceiling decorations and simplified the corner niches; we also designed the dark walnut tables with white gold leaf details. The master bedroom, which had been particularly dark in its previous incarnation, is now an airy refuge: walls, a headboard, and drapery of the same *gauffraged*, pearl-colored velvet continues the apartment's dominant palette while subtly differentiating the private space.

For the living room and dining room, Fisher Weisman designed complementary carpets incorporating outlines of motifs drawn from antique Serapi rugs; in the living room the abstracted outline is in chocolate brown and the field is cream; in the dining room, the colors are reversed, providing a subtly classical note that transitions well to a modern space. The living room incorporates vintage pieces as well—a brass, Chinese-style Italian armchair from the 1950s and Venetian sconces from the 1940s. The shell-encrusted side table is a bespoke piece by Fisher.

Above: A pair of Biedermeier chairs with a unique shape punctuates the main hallway; they convey age but have crisp, modern lines suited to the owners' contemporary tastes.

Opposite: Fisher Weisman designed a pair of demilune chests in cerused oak to coordinate with—and literally blend into—the paneling pattern of the living room walls.

Walnut and white gold leaf on both custom tables add subtle texture and interest to a dining room, while a silk Fortuny chandelier and Henri Matisse lithographs add more vibrant focal points.

The cabinetry in the kitchen was designed to integrate with the millwork that can be seen elsewhere in the apartment, particularly in the dining room, which is separated by a set of massive paneled pocket doors.

Continuing the apartment's overall monochromatic theme, the master bedroom's walls, drapery, and headboard are created from the same striated fabric.

NAPA VALLEY RESIDENCE
ST. HELENA, CALIFORNIA

This structure was built in the 1880s as a winery, abandoned for decades, and then renovated as a residence in the 1980s. The setting, the gardens, and the charm of the stone building were clearly positives—but nothing inside was salvageable.

We designed and oversaw a complete renovation, in which we rethought every detail inside the original structure's walls. The basic layout of the ground floor remained intact except for the kitchen—expanded by opening up several smaller rooms. Limed walnut millwork as well as deeply coffered ceilings add tactility and a sense of age. The coffers also serve the functional purpose of accommodating plumbing from upstairs without a need to lower the ceilings or to penetrate the stone structure. We designed massive walnut-and-ebony doors with an antique Portuguese feel and custom hardware to stand up to the stone structure and Venetian plaster interior surfaces.

Our scheme for the living room was meant to encourage evening and winter entertaining, when the hosts are compelled to keep guests indoors. While large enough to hold a good-sized party, the room is also cozy for one or two people. Portuguese-inspired corner banquettes are particularly conducive to reading and informal dining. We removed an awkward clerestory dormer, lightened the tone of the wood ceiling, and replaced a bland fireplace with a massive chimneypiece in walnut and antique mirror that is both dignified and whimsical.

We designed a curving staircase to give the entryway new life. An extension of the dormer in the master bedroom and bath and the removal of walls between small rooms on the upper level transform the private spaces into a grand master suite that includes a study, a bedroom, two dressing rooms, and a gracious bath.

A view into the living room is framed by stone walls from the original winery structure that date to the 1880s.

Above and opposite: The focal point of the living room is a massive custom mantel made of walnut and an antique mirror. A pair of antique iron *tazzas* featuring handles shaped like vipers rest on illuminated columns that flank the fireplace.

In the library, a boldly coffered ceiling in limed walnut adds historic character. The Fisher Weisman–designed sofa is upholstered in a vibrant mohair and the small bronze One Drink table is by Andrew Fisher.

Above: Specially designed Portuguese-inspired banquettes anchor two corners of the living room. In one, a dining table and two chairs create an intimate space for informal meals.

Opposite: In the formal dining room, an eighteenth-century Italian gilt-wood reliquary flanks the doorway to the kitchen. A grid of ebony tracery gives the doors a bold, rustic feel; the motif continues throughout the house, and Fisher Weisman even designed the pot rack beyond to echo its form.

Limed walnut cabinets and a white marble countertop are designed to complement the rough beauty of the house's original stone walls. Cabinets are fronted with antique mirror to add a bit of glamour and to bring more light into the room.

Above: An elliptical Portuguese-style partners' desk was the designers' solution for a study that needed shared workspace.

Opposite: A redesigned, airy staircase opens up the house's entryway and reinforces the theme of historic materials, such as wrought iron, found elsewhere throughout the house.

Above and opposite: The master bath incorporates spacious walnut cabinets and figured brown marble. The double shower incorporates an original exterior wall; its two high, original windows were perfectly placed to provide light as well as privacy. The wall of clear glass gives the shower—and the entire bathroom—an expansive feel.

SONOMA RESIDENCE
HEALDSBURG, CALIFORNIA

This compound in California wine country took over ten years to complete. First came the pool and pool house, followed by a one-of-a-kind tree house, where we occasionally slept on hot nights; next we planted a pinot noir vineyard, an olive orchard, and a large rose garden. Only with all of that complete did we begin work on the main house. Having become so familiar with the property, we knew exactly what we wanted to build: an airy one-bedroom house with a studio, a library, and several indoor and outdoor spaces for cooking and entertaining. Working with Tichenor & Thorp Architects, we created a contemporary structure that echoed the symmetry of classical pavilion architecture and had dashes of whimsy throughout.

The interior is a modest 2,500 square feet but feels much larger, thanks to an enfilade connecting the rooms along one side of the house, creating a sight line through the length of the building that exaggerates its scale. High ceilings and large windows add to the effect. Planked floors of white oak reclaimed from a nineteenth-century Pennsylvania barn laid throughout the house provide a warm, well-burnished ground for the otherwise crisp interiors.

The grandly proportioned living room is perfect for both large cocktail parties as well as for two people watching the home theater we discreetly hid behind a large, mixed-media folding screen. The kitchen is an inviting room for social gatherings and for entertaining on a grand scale, with its abundant storage and counter space and a built-in grill just behind the range. A large studio—in lieu of a family room—provides ample space for working on various projects. The library is a jewel of a compact space, with a spectacular bronze and olive-burl desk designed by Andrew and the best view in the house through enormous triple-hung windows. The master suite is arranged as a series of rooms with generous spaces for sleeping, reading, bathing, and dressing. The circular master bath with its freestanding steel tub below a six-foot-tall, shell-encrusted chandelier and tub filler is the house's showstopper. But the true pièce de résistance is the landscape, which we embellished with a cantilevered rear terrace shaded by a massive awning inspired by the great tents of India that overlooks the Russian River and vineyards.

Above: Andrew Fisher created a fantasy chandelier encrusted with seashells, smoky quartz crystal beads, and vintage shattered-acrylic balls for the foyer.

Opposite: A cast resin snail by Tony Duquette and a pair of nineteenth-century Italian altar decorations refashioned into lamps sit on an eighteenth-century French fruitwood buffet. A pair of oyster shell sconces by Fisher Weisman and a nineteenth-century Japanese door painted with peonies adorn the wall above. The paneled doors are painted with a fantasy *faux-bois* finish.

Overleaf: In the living room, a mixed-media screen by Andrew Fisher conceals a home theater. The carpet is an antique Moroccan. The massive eighteenth-century Italian armoire in the hallway beyond serves as a coat closet for guests.

Above: Oak branches gathered from the surrounding property and replicated in forged steel become a left- and right-facing pair of sconces. Fisher added pieces of real bark and moss to complete the lifelike effect.

Opposite: A collection of favorite paintings surrounds an eighteenth-century sculpture of an Italian saint; the Spanish table below dates to the same period. A brightly colored antique Moroccan carpet accents the grouping.

Overleaf: One-arm sofas upholstered in linen velvet are designed specifically to fit this space. Slipper chairs covered in antique Indian saris of handwoven silk and 24-karat gold found during a trip to Rajasthan play off the colors in "Spring," a quilt of painted and cut coffee filters by Andrew Fisher that hangs on the far wall. The side tables with sculptural bronze legs and petrified wood tops are also by Andrew Fisher.

Above: The master bedroom's vestibule features a table with a bronze base and limestone top by Andrew Fisher and a collection of Napoleonic-era memorabilia. The wall panel is made from antique Fortuny fabric.

Opposite: Fisher's Acanthus Major desk in bronze and burled olive wood is the centerpiece of the library.

Overleaf: An antique French daybed with *trompe l'œil* side panels is a focal point in a studio space; its faux-wood tones harmonize well with the two-toned gold leaf top of Fisher's Jester side table. The carved entry doors were purchased in Rajasthan.

Above: Antique Japanese panels from a temple ceiling provide a pop of color in the kitchen/dining area. A nineteenth-century French *bronze doré* chandelier in the form of a basket of thistles hangs over a dining table; vintage dining chairs are covered in antique African Kuba cloth.

Opposite: Hand-carved mahogany in the form of intertwined tree trunks and a slab top of California bay laurel are unique features of a table custom-designed by Fisher. The Parsons-style kitchen island is made of walnut and French limestone—a bookcase faces the dining table while appliances line its other side. The cabinets are sandblasted and limed white oak.

Linen velvet and antique Thai batik fabric add texture and interest to a headboard. An Italian Empire writing table and a carved and painted wood lamp by James Mont from the 1950s create a small workspace on the side of the bed.

Above: Cantilevered concrete flooring provides an outdoor room a spectacular view of the Russian River Valley. A custom, Indian-inspired awning provides shade.

Opposite: All windows facing the front of the house feature a Tree of Life–patterned wooden window screen. An ornate, shell-encrusted chandelier doubles as the tub filler.

SONOMA POOL PAVILION
HEALDSBURG, CALIFORNIA

The idea behind the pared-down structure of this pool house was to create a compact weekend getaway with all the functionality of a stand-alone house, which this served as for a decade. Working with Richard Beard of BAR Architects, we created a symmetrical, 1,000-square-foot house with an open plan. Six pairs of French doors with transoms open the house to the garden year round and twelve-foot ceilings of white-painted redwood paneling enhance the airy feel. The one main room accommodates a king bed, a living room, and a full kitchen. A generous bath anchors one end of the structure, and a laundry and storage room anchors the other. A wisteria-covered pergola creates a grand outdoor dining room overlooking a pool virtually the same size as the house. Shaded gardens at the rear, under a grove of oak trees, offer cool spots for summer dining and afternoon reading.

From the shell-encrusted *torchères* beckoning swimmers into the pool and the formally arranged garden furniture to the unexpectedly dressy interior, the simplicity of the architecture proves the perfect foil for more elaborate decorations. With fabrics in fresh, vibrant colors and patterns, the light-filled house has a delightfully sophisticated style.

Above: Gravel, boxwood, and neatly pruned trees give this garden setting a European flavor. The three-tiered Japanese pagoda in the distance supports the hanging target of an Olympic-scale archery range.

Opposite: The shade garden behind the pool pavilion provides an area for dining and lounge seating around a decorative fish pool.

SONOMA TREE HOUSE
HEALDSBURG, CALIFORNIA

What began as an idea to create an intimate, simple folly in a magnificent pair of ancient fir trees quickly became much more grand when arborists revealed how large a platform the trees could actually support.

On a nearly 30-by-30-foot deck, we were able to create a rather substantial, permanent structure to function as both guest cottage and art studio. The 400-square-foot interior space sits within a U-shaped porch, offering views in three directions. The fourth side of the structure houses utilities including, to the surprise of visitors, a fully plumbed water closet. As the structure was going up we found two pairs of Indian doors, one rustic and one fanciful Victorian complete with a lacy transom and original colored-glass panes, that easily became the focal point. The latter's unusual height in turn mandated the dramatic height of the tree house walls. We further exaggerated this height by incorporating a windowed cupola that vents hot air in the summer months.

The structure is a whimsical exercise in surprise and contrast: the exterior, clad in rustic redwood, blends into the natural setting of the trees as it ages, but the jewel-box interior uses glittering finishes and fabrics on the walls, windows, and furnishings to delight guests. To further the sense of amusement, a zip line off one side offers a quick escape.

Above: Victorian-era Indian teak doors and a transom with its original colored glass panels found in San Francisco were the first decorative elements introduced to the tree house. The dining table, created by Andrew Fisher, has a shell-encrusted base and gilded wood top and foot. Antique Chinese tree trunk stools with gilded tops provide thematically appropriate seating for guests.

Opposite: Vintage fauteuils were reimagined by Andrew Fisher with seashells and *faux-bois* painting on both their frames and silk upholstery. The floors are fir, the same species of tree in which the house is perched.

Above: Silk velvet and *trompe l'œil* finishes that suggest bird's-eye maple and tortoise lend distinction to a daybed that converts to a queen-size bed to accommodate overnight guests. An antique Chinese doll serves as a lamp's base.

Opposite: The interior scale is dramatized by floor-to-ceiling drapery and a pair of gilded steel twig light fixtures whose branches extend down from a 16-foot-high cupola.

Above: A vintage Chinese chest that conceals a sink sits below a whimsical paned window with colored glass panels that provides close-up views of the trees. A scooped side chair with a leather cushion continues the woodsy theme with a *faux-bois* finish. A pair of antique Indian carved doors leads to the veranda.

Opposite: Folding Syrian teak lounge chairs with bone inlay and a bronze One Drink table by Andrew Fisher beckon guests to the tree house's outdoor space.

NOB HILL PENTHOUSE
SAN FRANCISCO, CALIFORNIA

This penthouse, in one of San Francisco's most prestigious buildings, was skillfully renovated by Julia Morgan in the 1940s. Our clients fell in love with the classic Beaux-Arts floor plan and detailing, and hired us to update its infrastructure and to create a luxurious interior that would highlight their extensive collection of art and antiques. When we asked them to choose one word that would describe their ideal interior, they responded "exquisite." That single word laid the groundwork for the entire decorative scheme.

The central hall had bedrooms along one side and service areas tucked along the other. We converted the two bedrooms here, one of which Morgan had already transformed into a library, into his-and-hers studies. We converted the smaller of two master bedrooms into a second master dressing room. A former maid's room on the service side became their assistant's office—command central for the clients' busy lives.

The hall culminates in a second library, a semi-elliptical space elegantly designed by Morgan. From there, doors lead to the master suite, the living and dining rooms, and the kitchen. We furnished the dining room as a third library to house their extensive collection of antique books and *objets*, and to function as a home theater.

The original *boiserie* and hardware were meticulously restored and hand glazed. State-of-the-art lighting, automated sun control panels, audio/visual systems, and climate control were subtly incorporated into the fabric of the interior as well. The clients' love of warm colors resulted in a rich golden background that successfully sets off their astonishing collection of art and antiques.

Above: Renowned architect Julia Morgan, who had previously renovated this apartment, employed clever devices to create symmetrical pairs of small doors in the entry, including fashioning a single door that appears to be a pair when closed.

Opposite: In a previous renovation, Morgan created a jewel of a library in what had been a bedroom awkwardly placed just inside the front door. Fisher Weisman restored the limed oak paneling and added shutters to the bay window.

Above and opposite: A semi-elliptical library designed by Julia Morgan adds interest to a hall between the foyer and the living room. The owners' antique books and artwork collections fill the space.

Overleaf: Glazed millwork and paneling covered with grass cloth update a living room's traditional detailing. Groupings of striking African masks divide the boldly striped silk taffeta drapery.

Above and opposite: Modern art fills the living room. A painting over the fireplace by Jean Dubuffet, a bronze sculpture by Henri Matisse, and a drawing by Willem de Kooning live harmoniously inside the penthouse's Beaux-Arts shell.

The apartment's original dining room is now converted to a distinctive library and media room. Original paneling was glazed and its panels upholstered with a velvet in precisely the same shade of red to create a cocooning, cozy environment. Tall, custom, lacquered bookcases house antique books—the clients have an extensive collection—and decorative objects. A large home theater is concealed in the red lacquer cabinet at left.

Above: A Pablo Picasso woodblock print hangs over a Regency table in a corner of the red library.

Opposite: A collection of rare antique snuffboxes and an antique Chinese brazier fill a coffee table's surface. The painting over the fireplace is by Sean Scully and the life-sized bronze torso is by Manuel Neri.

Overleaf: In a light-filled master bedroom, a four-poster bed defines the space while important works of art, like a Robert Graham sculpture between the windows, punctuate the perimeter.

Above: A painting by Edouard Vuillard hangs over an ebonized chest; the deeply carved forms of both the chest and frame punctuate the room and visually anchor the bed.

Opposite: An oversized mirror above the apartment's original mantel amplifies the perception of space and light.

CARMEL RESIDENCE
CARMEL, CALIFORNIA

This home was the result of a happy collaboration between a talented architect, Heidi Hansen, and clients with great taste and the dream of building an improbably chic and sophisticated townhouse in the Carmel woods, on a gentle rise surrounded by beautiful trees. Spare lines and exquisite trim details make it both disciplined and elegant.

The decorative scheme is paced to create a shift of dynamics between the various rooms and the two distinct floors. The entry feels almost monastically minimalist until you take a moment to absorb the details: Louis XV *bronze doré* sconces frame the doors to the living room and dining room, and a dramatic lantern found at the Paris flea market peeks down from the dome over a gracefully curving staircase featuring a lyrical, hand-wrought bronze rail.

The dining room is dressy but restrained; its neutral background changes with the flowers and guests that fill it. The living room has velvet-upholstered walls, boldly patterned silk drapery, and intense jewel-tone silk velvets on chairs and pillows that create an enchanting background for entertaining. The kitchen and butler's pantry are warm and chic with wood floors, lightly cerused walnut cabinetry, a handsome table that functions as an island, honed gray stone counters, and shagreen-pattern wallcovering. The adjacent bay window easily accommodates the extended family for weekend breakfasts.

Upstairs the mood is decidedly lighter, where dark wood floors transition to soft wool carpeting and the fabrics shift from saturated to fresh hues. Icy silk taffeta drapery in the master bedroom complements the light colors of the bedding fabrics, and the master bath's crisp combination of white and lilac marble is enhanced by a wall of mirror.

A very personal collection of antique and contemporary furniture and lighting adds a layer of interest to all the rooms and helps to create a sense that this house has been here for ages, when in fact it just arrived.

Above: Walls upholstered in taupe velvet immediately produce a sense of luxurious comfort in a living room. A reproduction eighteenth-century mirror, 1960s Laverne cocktail table, pair of Maison Jansen chairs, and Fisher's bronze-and-glass Hollyhock Major table come together to create a truly eclectic space.

Opposite: The view into the living room is flanked by Louis XV sconces of similar provenance but different form. A dove-gray doorway frames a view of an ethereal Tom Leaver oil painting and serves as a neutral foil to both the art and the vibrant furnishings in the room beyond.

Overleaf: A Louis XVI sofa is given new life with the addition of striped upholstery and Fisher's red-lacquered Cloud cocktail table as a companion.

Above: A kitchen island in the form of a table with curved legs and stretchers minimizes its mass to help keep the room feeling open; the custom-designed pot rack above continues the theme. Cabinets in lightly cerused walnut are accented with pale gray marble counters.

Opposite: The breakfast nook's large bay window extends out into the garden. A curved banquette, Saarinen pedestal table, eighteenth-century Italian armchair, and vintage carved wood chandelier add decorative notes to the otherwise modernist space. Faux shagreen wall covering lends unexpected texture and interest.

Above: Herringbone-patterned white oak floors extend into the dining room, where a nineteenth-century French chandelier glows above a Maison Jansen mahogany-and-brass dining table and a suite of Louis XVI–style dining chairs. The finely detailed *boiserie* conceals generous closets in the corners.

Opposite: A butler's pantry contains luxurious touches such as walnut counters, antique mirror for the backsplash and upper cabinet door insets, and a fanciful 1940s Venetian lantern.

Above: In the master bedroom, Fisher's Acanthus Minor desk in burled myrtle wood and bronze serves as a bedside table; its intricately detailed pattern echoes that of the hand-quilted Fortuny bedspread nearby.

Opposite: A glimpse of the capacious dressing room as seen from the master bedroom.

The barrel-vaulted ceiling of the master bath recalls a Pompeiian villa, and the midcentury Venetian chandelier and complementary sconces complete the subtly Italian theme. Occupants of the freestanding tub have the enviable choice of facing either the woods outside or the wood-burning fireplace inside.

CASA ACANTO
SAN MIGUEL DE ALLENDE, MEXICO

On our very first visit to San Miguel de Allende, we realized our dream of owning a home in Mexico. The house we found, originally built as a tannery in the eighteenth century, had amazing bones and a large garden dominated by three enormous jacaranda trees. In addition, it sat on a surprisingly large piece of land in an ideal part of the old city, now a UNESCO World Heritage site.

Most houses of the era were built around a central courtyard designed to shut out the surrounding city, which today can feel claustrophobic. This house, however, was constructed along the top and side of a sloping, walled-in garden. The result was that every room opened to irresistible light and views.

Everything in the interior and much of the exterior is new: we preserved the structure of the house, but nothing of historical integrity remained and later renovations were not of interest. Working with outstanding craftsmen, we chose hand-hewn pine beams to add character and strength to the ceilings, designed new plaster and stone details, laid new tile floors that are hand-tinted with a combination of gasoline and tar to look well burnished, redesigned all the bathrooms and the kitchen, and had wood-plank doors crafted from reclaimed pine beams to create our vision of what the house wanted to be in the twenty-first century.

Working with architect Sebastián Zavala, we added an outdoor living room with stone arches and a wood-burning fireplace with an Argentinian grill. Above this, we gained a terrace adjoining the master bedroom. An unused section of the rooftop suggested itself for a guest room and bath. We also built a three-level casita by the pool that features another outdoor living room, two guest suites and baths, and a roof terrace with a 360-degree view of the city.

We combined favorite furniture, artwork, fabrics, lighting, and objects collected over the years with new pieces we designed specifically for the house. Long fans of blue-and-white color schemes, we used many shades of each to create our vision of Mexican beauty.

Above and opposite: The designers added a vaulted ceiling and reclaimed eighteenth-century stone pavers to this entrance hall. These carved cantera stone brackets with an acanthus leaf motif echo the name of the house, Casa Acanto. The runner is antique Moroccan.

Above and opposite: Harnessing local talent, Fisher worked with Mexican artisans to create special blue-and-white tiles for a frieze that runs along the top of the kitchen walls. Cabinet doors are built from reclaimed pine beams and framed in sabino wood. The mass of the oven hood is minimized by an unexpected use of mirror. The center table, with drawers on both sides for extra storage capacity, is composed of a mesquite slab top and bronze legs. The chandelier is nineteenth-century French *bronze doré*.

Above: The breakfast room opens directly onto the patio and an outdoor living room.

Opposite: An antique French dining table accommodates up to six for simple dinners in the kitchen. The armoire at right was designed in a unique way—its large central door conceals a "secret" passageway to the art studio and garage beyond. A fireplace added to the far wall is flanked by a pair of comfortable tub chairs, and the chandelier over the seating arrangement was a copper incense burner in a former life.

Overleaf: The dining room is dominated by a massive shell-encrusted chandelier by Fisher Weisman; it hovers above their Cipresso table and a set of Irish Hall chairs. The designers replaced the existing mantel with a version in dramatically carved cantera stone, and allow a vintage mirror created by an artist from Mexico City to serve as a dramatic overmantel. Fisher crafted the candelabra from a pair of andirons, adding faux coral armatures and strings of crystal beads.

Above and opposite: New niches in an unconventional-yet-familiar shape loosely echo the design of the dining room's chandelier. Mesquite-wood chests with curved fronts are custom-designed to fit exactly below these spaces, and are paired with lamps fashioned from antique copper urns. The hand-carved mahogany base of the Cipresso table and the curved bases of the Irish Hall chairs complement the curvaceous, exotic chandelier.

Overleaf: An outdoor living room fitted with generously cushioned seating from the designers' Arcadia collection and marble cocktail tables made in Rajasthan functions as the primary entertaining space. A wood-burning fireplace with a built-in Argentinean grill anchors the space.

A large quilt of painted coffee filters by Andrew Fisher and a pair of custom mesquite wood bookcases occupy a broad living room wall. Carved and painted lamps by James Mont dating to the 1950s provide lighting for the spacious banquette and daybeds on bronze legs. Custom tabourets upholstered in Indian silk-and-peacock-feather fabric are topped with turned discs of California bay laurel and sit on a pair of antique Moroccan carpets, reinforcing the circular and patchwork themes of Fisher's art.

Above: An eclectic but symmetrical assortment of objects and artwork surrounds an eighteenth-century French fruitwood buffet.

Opposite: A cantera stone mantel and its handwoven steel screen were made by local artisans. A mixed-media, four-panel screen by Fisher, above, opens to reveal a home theater. A pair of small eighteenth-century Spanish chairs with leather seats and backs completes the vignette of artisanally crafted items.

The dining terrace benefits from the shade of a canopy of jacaranda trees.

Above and opposite: Overlooking the lower garden, with its massive cantera stone fountain, pool, and casita, a dining terrace awaits guests.

Above: Fisher Weisman designed a dramatic fountain in stone and antique mirror for the dining terrace. Water flows out of a bronze acanthus leaf sculpted by Fisher and down into a fern that sits in a large, fluted oval urn of carved stone. Rivulets of water flow from it into the pool below.

Opposite: The designers opened a stair completely, freeing it from claustrophobic masonry walls by adding a stone column to support the landing above. A whimsical iron rail mimics a twisted velvet rope, complete with tassels.

Above: Spanish-style furniture, drapery, and a custom-upholstered chair in blue and white reinforce the house's main color scheme and reference its location. The small bronze table is one of a trio designed by Fisher Weisman.

Opposite: A guest bath features high ceilings, a tile wainscot, and partial walls topped with fanciful plaster scrolls. The large, open shower looks out onto a private terrace.

Upholstered pieces in the master bedroom—headboard, lounge chair, and ottoman—are united by linen velvet trimmed in antique Thai batik linen. The settee at the foot of the bed is 1930s French and is upholstered in a hand-loomed silk velvet ikat the designers purchased in Istanbul. Warm colors from the antique Moroccan rug are picked up in the artwork by Andrew Fisher.

Above: Fisher Weisman designed a dark-stained, drop-front desk for the master bedroom. The upper doors fold back to reveal a large television and an air-conditioning unit. The ikat drapery is made of a handwoven silk-and-cotton fabric purchased on a trip to Istanbul.

Opposite: Original domed brick and exterior stone give a historic feeling to the study. A gilded tapestry by Fisher overlooks the room. A nineteenth-century French wing chair is updated with Turkish silk ikat; it sits next to a nineteenth-century French gueridon.

Above: The domed, oval-shaped master bathroom is fitted with a copper chandelier that doubles as a novelty faucet for filling the copper bathtub below. The walls are patterned with a traditional Mexican border tile arranged in a way that creates symmetrical stripes.

Opposite: A sabino wood vanity follows the curve of the oval space and is inset into the wall. With the help of a local foundry, the designers created the cast bronze faucet.

A new three-level casita adds a
second outdoor living room, two
bedrooms, two baths, and a roof
terrace with a panoramic view of
the property. The pool is lined with
cobalt-blue tiles accented with a
mosaic of gold glass.

The historic home is organized around a sloping, central garden that tumbles genteelly down a hillside.

Overleaf: The view from the casita's roof terrace looks over the UNESCO World Heritage–designated city.

ACKNOWLEDGMENTS

We have had the amazing good fortune through the years of working with the best of the best.

We are especially thankful to Margaret Russell, Pilar Viladas, Lou Gropp, Stanley Abercrombie, Mayer Rus, Marian McEvoy, Dominique Browning, Michael Boodro, Dara Caponigro, and Newell Turner for featuring our projects in their publications and providing us with a national audience.

We are indebted to Grey Crawford, Tim Street-Porter, François Dischinger, Matthew Millman, David Duncan Livingston, Edmund Barr, and Simon Watson for the extraordinary images they have crafted of our work. Their skillful documentation has been essential to communicating our style through the years—in the press and in these pages.

It has been our privilege to work with extraordinarily gifted architects including Tichenor & Thorp Architects, Andrew Skurman Architects, Richard Beard/BAR Architects, Heidi Hansen, and DomA Architects. Our collaboration with each of these firms has been rich.

Producing the range of custom designs that forms the core of our work requires an army of highly skilled and passionate artisans. Karin Wikström has executed most of our decorative finishes while Robinson Finishes, Ltd. and Stancil Studios have each added their unique touch. Jane Babinski of Architrave and Dawson Custom Workroom have provided superb sewing. J.F. Fitzgerald, Hilde-Brand Furniture, Inc., Parenteau Studios in Chicago, and Urban-Delta LLC of New York have beautifully crafted our custom upholstery. Our indispensable source for extraordinary reclaimed and custom milled wood slabs is Evan Shively of Arborica. Julian Giuntoli Custom Furniture, San Francisco Custom Furniture, and Thomas Sellars Furniture have built our wood furniture while JAFE Custom Finishing and Rossi Antiques have added fine finishes. Rossi is also our go-to source for restoration and reproduction. Finally, Paul Ferrante, Inc. and Dogfork Lamp Arts create most of our custom lighting designs, for which La Bella Copia hand makes perfect lamp shades.

Creating furniture and lighting for leading manufacturers has been a rewarding extension of our interior design work. The lion's share of this effort has been with Michael Taylor Designs, which has produced a tremendous range of our interior and garden furniture designs over the past two decades. We have also created wicker, teak, and lighting designs for The Wicker Works and Walters Wicker, and unexpected lighting designs for Boyd Lighting and The Kentfield Collection. Thank you for being great partners and for giving us the opportunity to offer our designs to a wider public.

We have been fortunate to have many talented young designers in our studio over the years. In particular we applaud Arcadia Smails, Bryn Brugioni, Daniel O'Neill, Yenni Setiawan, and Whitney Mendelsohn. It has been our pleasure to have each of you be part of Fisher Weisman.

To these talented firms and individuals and the many more we have met and been inspired by along the way, thank you.

PHOTOGRAPHY CREDITS

Principal photography by Grey Crawford

David Duncan Livingston: 5, 8

Matthew Millman: 10, 12, 94, 96–113

Tim Street-Porter: 30, 32–39

François Dischinger: 82, 84–93

Edmund Barr: 142, 144–149

Copyright © 2013 by The Monacelli Press, LLC.
All rights reserved. Published in the United States by The Monacelli Press, LLC.

Fisher, Andrew
Artful decoration : interiors by Fisher Weisman/Andrew Fisher & Jeffry Weisman—First edition.
pages cm
ISBN 978-1-58093-358-2 (hardcover)
1. Fisher Weisman (Firm)
2. Interior decoration—United States.
I. Weisman, Jeffry. II. Title.
NK2004.3.F57F57 2013
747—dc23   2012034266

10 9 8 7 6 5 4 3 2 1

First edition

Printed in China

Designed by Carrie Hunt

www.monacellipress.com